DAREDEVIL SPORTS

PAINTBALL

By Demi Jackson

Gareth Stevens
PUBLISHING

HOT TOPICS

Please visit our website, www.garethstevens.com. For a free color catalog of all our high-quality books, call toll free 1-800-542-2595 or fax 1-877-542-2596.

Jackson, Demi.
Paintball / by Demi Jackson.
p. cm. — (Daredevil sports)
Includes index.
ISBN 978-1-4824-2992-3 (pbk.)
ISBN 978-1-4824-2989-3 (6 pack)
ISBN 978-1-4824-2991-6 (library binding)
1. Paintball (Game) — Juvenile literature. I. Title.
GV1202.S87 J335 2016
796.2—d23

First Edition

Published in 2016 by
Gareth Stevens Publishing
111 East 14th Street, Suite 349
New York, NY 10003

Designer: Samantha DeMartin
Editor: Kristen Rajczak

Photo credits: Cover, p. 1 Fotokvadrat/Shutterstock.com; p. 5 Pavel L Photo and Video/Shutterstock.com; p. 7 Peter Dazeley/The Image Bank/Getty Images; p. 9 kravka/Shutterstock.com; pp. 11, 13, 24, 29 Dmitry Kalinovsky/Shutterstock.com; pp. 14, 15 Jasminko Ibrakovic/Shutterstock.com; p. 17 Joe Raedle/Getty Images Sport/ Getty Images; p. 19 Igor Berlinskiy/Shutterstock.com; pp. 21, 25 © iStockphoto.com/ Ibrakovic; p. 23 Richard Jary/Shutterstock.com; p. 27 grafvision/Shutterstock.com.

Printed in the United States of America

CPSIA compliance information: Batch #CS15GS: For further information contact Gareth Stevens, New York, New York at 1-800-542-2595.

CONTENTS

THE LINE OF FIRE

Splat! Bright yellow paint hits the tree you're hiding behind. You peek out to see who shot at you. Quickly, you ready your paintball gun and fire back. Your **opponent** is hit—and out of the game!

RISK FACTOR

Anyone can learn to play paintball! Players under ages
18 or 16 may need a parent to say it's OK to play.
Those under 10 may need a parent present.

In paintball, one team works to eliminate, or get out, another team by shooting balls of paint at them. Once a player is hit, or marked, they're out of the game. Often the goal is to take the other team's flag, like in capture the flag.

RISK FACTOR

Paintballs are small **capsules** full of colored liquid. The capsules have a thin skin so they break easily.

GET THE GEAR

Paintball has really cool gear! Each player has a paintball gun, or marker, that uses **compressed** air to shoot paintballs. Some will keep shooting paintballs as long as there's a finger on the trigger. Others have to be pumped in order to shoot.

RISK FACTOR

For safety reasons, paintball guns have limits on how fast and how far they can shoot paintballs. Most guns shoot at speeds less than 300 feet (91 m) per second.

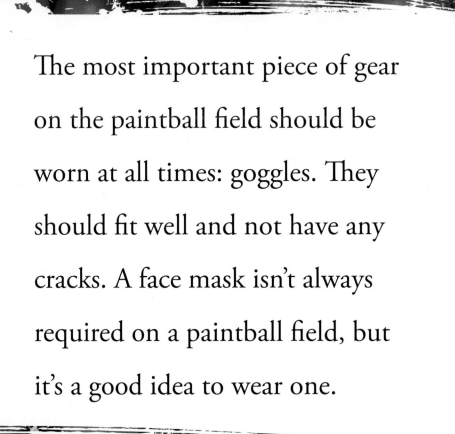

The most important piece of gear on the paintball field should be worn at all times: goggles. They should fit well and not have any cracks. A face mask isn't always required on a paintball field, but it's a good idea to wear one.

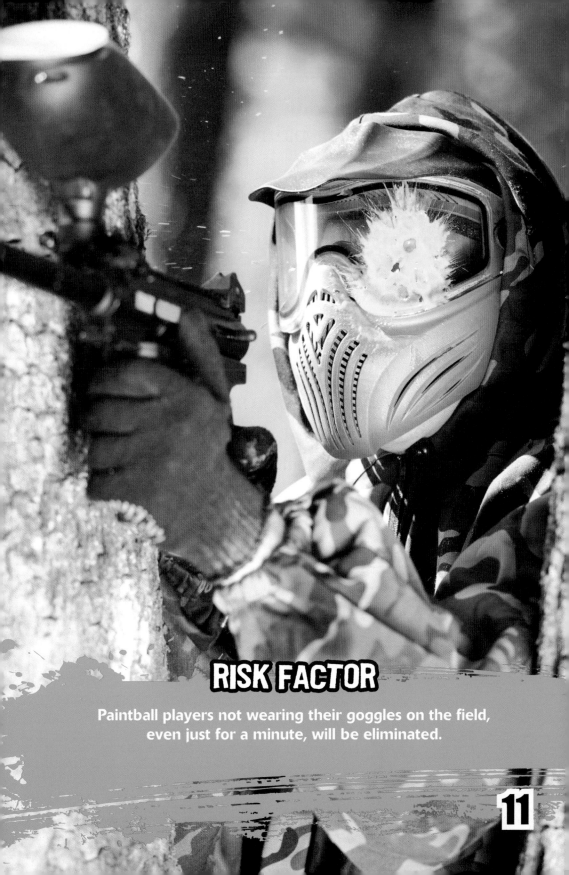

RISK FACTOR

Paintball players not wearing their goggles on the field,
even just for a minute, will be eliminated.

When playing paintball, wear pants and a long-sleeve shirt or sweatshirt. Make sure you can move well and aren't wearing bright colors that will make you stand out too much. Players commonly wear boots or sneakers so they can run on uneven ground.

RISK FACTOR

Loose-fitting clothing makes it a little harder for a paintball to break on you.

13

WOODSBALL

Woodsball is a kind of paintball mostly played outside. These paintball fields are built around naturally occurring trees, hills, and open areas. The first people to play games of paintball in the early 1980s played woodsball.

RISK FACTOR

Paintball games can have as few as 2 people or more than 200. It all depends on how big the field is.

SPEEDBALL

If you're playing on a level field or indoors, you're probably playing speedball. There are **bunkers** on the field to hide behind. Speedball paintball games are usually quicker and use more paintballs.

RISK FACTOR

Most paintball games last under an hour, but some special games can be as long as a day!

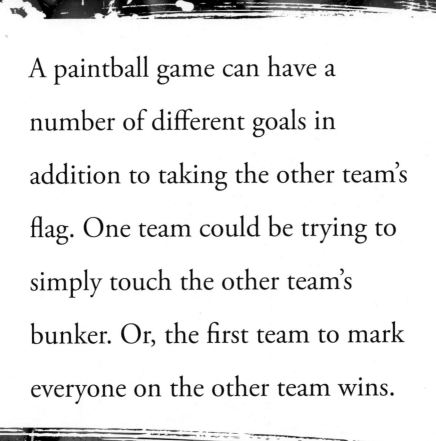

A paintball game can have a number of different goals in addition to taking the other team's flag. One team could be trying to simply touch the other team's bunker. Or, the first team to mark everyone on the other team wins.

RISK FACTOR

No matter what kind of paintball you're playing, there should be no body contact between players.

FOLLOW THE RULES

There are no set rules that apply to every paintball game. Each field will have some different rules. One common rule requires players to cover or plug their markers when not playing a game.

RISK FACTOR

Before starting a paintball game, always be sure there are enough **referees** for the number of players. For example, one referee isn't nearly enough for a 50-player game!

The top rule of paintball game play is that hitting another player eliminates them. If the paintball doesn't break, that player stays in. However, it's a common rule that if a player calls "I'm hit!" before knowing they aren't marked, they're still out.

RISK FACTOR

Some fields only count a mark if it's on a person's body or legs. Shots to the head or marker won't count.

Many paintball fields have a **surrender** rule. If a player finds an opponent who doesn't notice they've been caught, the player should ask for surrender once they're about 15 feet (4.6 m) apart. This keeps anyone from getting hit at close range.

RISK FACTOR

Overshooting is when one player shoots another many times in a row. This is commonly against the rules.

OUCH!

Getting hit by a paintball *does* hurt. It's often compared to how it feels when a rubber band is snapped against your skin. You're likely to leave a game of paintball with a few scratches from running around the field, too.

RISK FACTOR

Compared to other sports, the number of
injuries in paintball is quite low!

WORKING TOGETHER

You can play paintball with all your friends! Beginners can play with those who have played a lot and still have a good time. Working together as a paintball team is a great way to try something that takes a little daring!

RISK FACTOR

Do you want to play paintball?
There are fields all over the country!

SAFETY TIPS
ALL PAINTBALL PLAYERS SHOULD:

- stay fit by being active.

- wear goggles and a face mask.

- keep their paintball gun covered or plugged when it's not in use.

- never look into their paintball gun.

- know and follow the rules of each paintball field.

- bring water to drink after a game.

FOR MORE INFORMATION

BOOKS

Otfinoski, Steven. *Extreme Paintball*. New York, NY: Marshall Cavendish, 2013.

Power, Bob, and Greg Roza. *Sports Tips, Techniques, and Strategies: An Insider's Guide to Paintball*. New York, NY: Rosen Publishing, 2014.

WEBSITES

Learn Basic Paintball Tactics
www.ehow.com/video_2365787_learn-basic-paintball-tactics.html
Watch this video and link to many others about how to play paintball well.

Top Ten Paintball Tips and Tricks
paintball.about.com/od/strategy/tp/paintball_tips.htm
Become a better paintball player using these tips.

GLOSSARY

bunker: something in the way on a paintball field including a building, a big pile of logs, or a cloth shape filled with air

capsule: a sac enclosing something

compressed: pressed or squeezed together

opponent: the person or team you must beat to win a game

referee: an official who makes sure players follow the rules

surrender: to give up

INDEX